The Watcher in the Lighthouse

Written and Illustrated by Tom Romano

Published by AB Film Productions
290 West 12th St.
New York, NY 10014
abfilm 9@gmail.com

telephone: 212-741-1441

©2017 Tom Romano, all rights reserved

ISBN: 978-0-997-1715-2-5

Dedicated to my mom who was always there for me. She was, and continues to be, an inspiration.

Rue walked quietly through the house. This evening she wanted to peek into bedrooms to see what people were doing. Sometimes, if she ran into someone out in the hall she'd smile and nod; the response was people walking past her as though she wasn't there.

Mostly she didn't want to let anyone know where she was, so she observed people from a distance. Occasionally she would watch a group of people in the living room, shaking her head and wondering why there were so many strangers in her house.

"What happened to everyone I used to see here?" she wondered. She looked out the window. In the parking area were horseless carriages. She'd heard of them, but where were the buggies she remembered? There were metal numbered plates attached to each horseless carriage.

That afternoon she was in the attic looking through a chest of drawers. The top two drawers were empty, but the third one down had trouble opening, as though something was blocking it. Pulling it open, she reached inside, and felt something wedged against the back part of the chest. Carefully she pried it loose. A child's doll. A Raggedy Ann she'd made herself. There was something stuck into the back of the doll. Rue reached in and pulled out a small book. The title page had a dedication, and she leaned in close to see what it was. "To our daughter Chrissie on her ninth birthday," read the worn, faded scrawl. She turned the page.

May 16 Found five violets today. Spring is here!

There was another date and entry. She started to read it, stopped, and the attic began spinning around her. Closing her eyes, time slipped slowly away as she remembered a conversation from long, long ago.

"I meant it, Charles. Please be careful."

"Well, must go to work. That was a delicious dinner."

Chrissie sat quietly, cradling her doll.

"They're talking about a storm tonight," Rue said.

Her handsome, bearded husband laughed. Charles had his blue lightkeeper's uniform on.

"We'll be careful." He kissed his wife goodbye.

"I don't think this place could operate without the head lightkeeper," Rue said.

Charles picked up a kerosene lantern, left the house, and trudged up the hill.

He smiled at some children playing in the yard. Nearby chickens clucked and scolded,

scratching for beetles and grubs in the ground. One little boy looked at him curiously.

"Going to the lighthouse?"

Charles smiled. "Yes, it's time for the lamp to be lit." He stopped and gazed up the hill at the lighthouse. It flashed after dark every day of the year, sending beams 21 miles out to sea. The light warned passing ships that they must stay clear of the dangerous shoals and rocks below.

"I need to look in on the horses and cows," said Charles to himself. A long, white building appeared in the fading light. Charles undid the latch and peeked in to where the chickens would have to go in their coop after dark; there were too many raccoons, skunks, and owls that would be after them.

Charles reached the lighthouse and stared at the sky. Usually he liked to look at the ocean with his telescope, to see if he could spy any ships. But tonight he was worried.

He reached into his pocket and pulled out the telegraphed note. "Storm imminent. Keep lighthouse going 24 hours for the next two days." That was all. He saw black clouds gathering around the setting sun. There were wispy clouds floating high up in the sky, and the sunset was a deeper orange than usual.

"Papa!" The voice came from behind him. Charles turned, and there was Chrissie.

"You forgot this!" she handed him a container. Charles swept his little daughter into his arms forgetting the danger for the moment. He knew the container had some food, as well as a book. Sometimes late at night, he would take time out from his tasks to read by lantern light.

Papa, can I stay with you?" pleaded Chrissie.

"Perhaps, for a little while. Then you'll need to go home to bed," said Charles.

"Is something bad going to happen tonight?"

Charles looked at Chrissie's anxious face and smiled.

"No, honey, everything is alright. If you stay with me a little while, I'll read to you. Then you must go back."

Charles stopped at a small storage building, one of three, next to the lighthouse. He unlocked it and stepped inside. A few minutes later he was back outside, carrying a heavy, dark can. It contained the coal oil (kerosene) needed to keep the light burning. He unlocked the door to the lighthouse, and went inside, Chrissie following.

"Can I help you wind the weight up?" asked Chrissie.

Charles saw the metal bar hanging a few inches from the ground. Someone had become too careless in allowing this. He set the drum of kerosene down and walked up the winding stairs to the light, and lit the wick in the center of the lens with a long match. Then he walked downstairs to the winding machine. Taking a deep breath, he began cranking the weight. He had to raise the weight all the way up three stories. It would pull the Fresnel lens around the light, magnifying and refracting its light into eight beams which would shoot out of the lighthouse in all directions. As soon as he began to crank the weight, the lens began turning.

5. Every few seconds a beam of light would sweep over the ocean. The only way a beam's light would end was due to the curvature of the earth. Charles remembered one of the last lightkeepers would set an "alarm" to tell him when to crank the weight up again. He'd go to sleep under the weight until it was touching his stomach!

Charles looked down at Chrissie. She was looking eagerly at him. He tried to imagine his little girl pulling a two hundred pound weight three flights to the top. Smiling, he raised the weight a third of the way and stopped. Arms aching, he reached into a cupboard, and took out two logbooks to record temperature and wind speed. The wind outside increased to a high, piercing whine.

"Papa, that sounds like someone crying!" said Chrissie.

Charles put the logbook down. Rain spattered against the window. The wind lessened for a minute or two then howled more loudly than before. Then they heard a sound like a ship's horn blasting away, echoing in the distance.

There was a knock on the lighthouse door. Charles ran down the stairs. The second and third assistant lightkeepers stood there.

"There's a ship aground at Devil's Elbow!" shouted one. "We need all the help we can get!"

Charles grabbed his coat and rushed upstairs. "Chrissie you must stay here! I'll be back in a little while."

Chrissie didn't want to stay in the lighthouse by herself.

"Can't I come with you, Papa? Just to watch?"

"No, Chrissie. You musn't go outside. The wind is blowing too hard. Just stay here until I return." Charles kissed his daughter and left.

Chrissie knew where Devil's Elbow Beach was. She'd gone there many times and played with other children. She waited until her papa's voice had died away, and grabbed her coat. "I've got to go out there. Maybe I can help," she thought. She opened the door, and was greeted by a big gust of wind. Pushing the door closed, she ran down the path. Far ahead were the lighted windows of the lightkeeper's houses. She ran faster, hoping no one would see her. Raindrops splattered onto her face and hair, but Chrissie ran on.

Finally, after what seemed an eternity, she ran past the barn, and the keeper's houses and headed down to the beach. She looked straight ahead, but it was too dark to see anything. As she neared the beach, the moon came out and she saw a small group of people standing near the water's edge. There was a listing steamer ship out in the water, it's mast atilt; it was pointing to the side rather than straight up.

"They must be the rescuers!" thought Chrissie.

They were holding something that looked like a long rope. The other end was way out in the water; swimmers were grabbing onto the rope and being pulled towards the beach. Chrissie stood under a tree watching. The wind whipped her hair and clothes around, but she didn't leave. An hour passed, and she had a sudden thought of going immediately back to the lighthouse. Papa would be angry that she'd disobeyed him and come all the way back to the keeper's houses by herself in the storm. She must get back to the lighthouse, now. She began walking quickly up the hill.

In ten minutes she was back at the lighthouse. She opened the door and walked in. Then she heard something strange, a grating noise. In the center of the room, Chrissie stopped and stared. The weight for the winding mechanism was only a foot above the ground! She ran to the crank but it was too high for her. Quickly she grabbed a box and placed it on the floor under the winding device and climbed onto it. This time her arms reached the crank, but when she tried rewinding, it wouldn't budge. Looking around the room, she wondered what to do. She must get back to the keeper's houses and get someone to help wind the weight back up. She knew she had to act fast, or it would hit the floor in a few minutes, and the lens would stop turning. Quickly she ran outside and down the path to the keeper's house. She went to the assistant keepers house first, but it was dark. Everyone must have gone to bed, she thought. She could still see the marooned vessel and rescuers on the beach far below, and knew her papa was still down there. Some of the lights in her house were still on; there were people downstairs.

Running there, she tried the backdoor; it was locked. She pounded furiously until the door opened, and there stood her mother with a kerosene lamp.

"Chrissie, why are you back here? I thought you were up at the lighthouse!" said Rue.

Chrissie was so paralyzed with fright she could barely speak.

"Mama, come quick! The weight for the lighthouse is almost all the way down! Papa is down at the beach and can't come!" cried Chrissie.

Rue stared for a moment toward the beach. "Dear God! He's probably forgotten about the light!" She grabbed her coat, threw it on over her night-dress, and went outside, slamming the door behind her. They hurried up to the lighthouse. Leaves blew across their path, and more wind-driven rain spattered onto their clothing as they struggled up the hill.

The light was still turning.

"Thank God!" said Rue. She quickly walked over to the winding mechanism and began cranking it. Her arms strained, but after a moment or two, the wheel began turning, pulling the weight up. Periodically she would stop to rest. It took Rue almost thirty minutes to crank the two hundred pound weight to the top. Finally she sat down. Suddenly they heard someone talking outside, followed by the sound of approaching footsteps.

The door opened, and there stood Charles, breathing hard. Starting to walk quickly towards the windup crank, he stopped when he saw his wife and daughter. Going to center of the room, he looked to see where the weight was.

"Did *you* wind it all the way up?" he asked Rue.

"Yes, I did, but you can thank your daughter for saving the light. She came and got me just in time."

Charles stared at Rue and then down at Chrissie, who was smiling by her side. "How close do you think it came to stopping?" he asked. "I was so intent on saving the sailors I couldn't think of anything else. I was timing when I'd need to crank the lens then I forgot," said Charles.

"It was a few inches above the floor. Probably would've stopped if Chrissie hadn't caught it."

Charles swept Chrissie into a bearhug, then kissed Rue. "You probably saved more ships and the lives of more sailors."

"Was everyone safe?" asked Rue.

"Thank heavens, yes, but the ship and its contents were lost. Near as I can understand, somebody wasn't paying attention in the pilothouse of that ship. It's rumoured he fell asleep at the steering wheel."

"Where is the captain and crew? Were there any passengers?"

"No. It was just a small cargo vessel with a captain and crew of six. They're staying at the assistant lightkeeper's house."

"Well, this night had a happy ending," said Rue.

"Yes, it did." Charles said, reaching for the logbooks. "Except I almost fell into that cistern. I was running down to the beach and decided to take a shortcut through the north woods. I've got to do something about making sure it has a higher wall around it. I'll take care of it this weekend."

Chrissie was excited. She had been part of an adventure and had saved the lives of people! She couldn't wait to tell her friends in school tomorrow. And she would tell her secret friend about it, too.

Chrissie had a little doll named Rags. Rags was a Raggedy Anne doll that Chrissie had had for a long time. She was Chrissie's "secret friend;" who would listen to her when she talked about teachers, or her parents. Chrissie liked Rags because she didn't talk back. However, there were moments when Chrissie wished the doll *could* talk. She would have asked for advice

11. from Rags when Chuck, a classmate of hers, pulled her hair. Chrissie wanted revenge.

"Well, what do you think I should do?" she asked Rags. Chrissie decided Rags didn't want to get involved; she'd better take things into her own hands. The next day at school she waited until Chuck's head was bent over his desk, then hit him with a wadded-up

piece of paper. Chrissie quickly folded her arms and looked innocently out the window. The teacher glanced up, but hadn't noticed anything; nor did her classmates. "It'll be our secret," she told Rags that evening. "No one knows what I did but us." Suddenly she felt bad about hitting

Chuck. "Did I do the wrong thing?" she asked Rags. The next day, during school recess, she put a flower in Chuck's desk. "He'll never know where it came from, but that's alright," she thought.

One day she asked her secret friend about the north woods. Charles and Rue had taken her there once, but it was dark where the trees grew close together. She didn't like its damp, heavy-scented odor. Since then, her parents had strictly forbidden her to go there alone. Still, sometimes she had thoughts of exploring it

"You don't want to go into those woods anyway," a boy had told her. "They're haunted. Ghosts lie in wait for someone like you, then grab you. A kid visiting ten years ago disappeared in there." Chrissie wondered if he was telling the truth. She shuddered, thinking about a spirit grabbing her.

Rue stared at the diary pages. Chrissie had loved to invent things. One day she was looking for the cookie jar in the kitchen. She didn't find any cookies, but she did find the white sugar used for baking. First she wet her face and arms, then sprinkled sugar all over them. Then she walked casually into the living room, where Rue, Charles, and Samuel were sitting. "I'm a cookie," she said.

There were several wet splotches on the diary pages, and looking closer, Rue realized they were her tears. She opened another page and began reading.

May 18. Found a robin's feather today. Lost another tooth.

There was another entry below it, very faded and partially obscured with mold.

We put another play on today.

Sometimes Chrissie had rounded up the other children and they would surprise the adults with an impromptu play. She would give the others a script, and they would find old clothes feathers, beads, or anything they could dress up in. The adults would be sitting in the living room, winking at one another and pretending they didn't know anything about missing bedspreads and blankets. In the next room Chrissie and the other children would be fussing with each other's costumes whispering about what they were going to do. (The adults could hear every word.)

"Where's Ned? He's supposed to be playing the chief."

Ned poked his head from behind the curtain made from a bedsheet.

"Uh, here I am."

Becky, a friend of Chrissie's, stamped her foot.

"Well, we can't start the play if they don't do the Indian war whoop," she said.

WOOOOO WOOOO WOOO! yelled the Indians.

"Start! Go!" said Becky, frantically, pushing Ned. Chief Ned went to take his place near Chrissie, and tripped over the curtain, landing in front of the audience with a loud "OOOOF." But just in time the handsome rescuer stepped in, grabbed the maiden, Chrissie, and pulled her toward his "stallion." The "horse" was a wheeled, black hobbyhorse with a broom tail and a scraggly, worn straw mane. The hero rescuer was a freckle-faced boy named Simon. Simon got Chrissie onto the horse, but then tripped over the horse's tail, falling backward onto the floor. Horse, maiden, and hero all fell together in a heap, and that was the end of the play. No one saw Becky slip into the kitchen and grab a pitcher of water. She poured it on Simon's head.

"Thanks for ruining everything," she hissed angrily.

"Hey, look everybody, I'm drowning," laughed Simon, taking it all in stride.

The adults cheered and clapped, not realizing this was not part of the act.

"The play was Chrissie's idea," Rue had said proudly to the others. "Isn't she clever?"

14.

Rue looked at the pages of the diary, blinking her eyes. A tightness like a vise gripped her bosom. She turned another page.

June 3   Mama and Papa took me to the beach today. We made a kite.

Rue remembered Chrissie scampering around on the sand, chasing tiny scuttling crabs or playing with other children. She remembered the kite made of paper and balsa wood sticks that Chrissie and she had spent an afternoon making. Rue had found an old watercolor box. They painted bright colors on it.

"Let's see how high we can fly it," Rue had said. They attached some string and let it soar high up into the sky, the colors flashing in the sunlight, until it was just a speck.

"Do you think we can fly it all the way to heaven?" asked Chrissie.

Rue smiled. "I don't know, maybe," she had said.

"Let's go down to the wet sand and build a sandcastle, " suggested Charles.

They found a spot and began molding the ramparts. Then up came a couple of towers followed by a wall.

"We need to build a moat," said Charles.

"Papa, is that where the king lives?" asked Chrissie, pointing to one of the towers.

"That's right. He sits all day counting his money," said Charles.

"And there's the queen's chambers, where she sits eating bread and honey," said Rue. After awhile the tide began running into the castle.

"The castle is flooding! We must rescue them," said Chrissie.

"They're actually already gone," said Charles. "The King has some fast horses. He did, however, leave his servants."

"Oh, they'll drown! We'd better get them out," said Chrissie, looking with dismay at the rising waters destroying their handiwork.

"Uh, huh." said Charles. He pretended to scoop something up from the sandcastle. "Here are the pretty maids all in a row. And there are the cooks, and, of course, the footsoldiers."

Charles picked up his fishing pole. "I'll be gone awhile," he said.

"Can I come with you?" asked Chrissie.

No, Chrissie, the water there is too dangerous. Maybe when you're older," said Charles.

He headed off to some rocks at the north end of the beach. Charles always brought back a fat rockfish or two for the cooking pot.

One time, Chrissie found a bright orange stone and put it in her pocket. She wondered what she should do with it. She thought of giving it to her secret friend, but didn't know what a doll would do with an orange stone. "She'd probably just stare at it," she thought. Her mother had told her, "Look for brightly colored stones. They're called agates. Who knows, maybe they came from some other world. They're very special, for you to keep."

Chrissie wasn't sure she should keep this one; it looked so beautiful. That night, she sneaked into her parents bedroom and placed it on their nightstand. The next morning, there was a note next to the agate that read, "although there are other mommies and daddies in the world, you're my favorite! I love you." She couldn't think of how to end the note but signed, "From the tooth fairy." She had loved the many visits from the tooth fairy and thought her parents would too.

June 12   Mama found out about the shoebox today.

Rue smiled. She turned the pages of the diary. One spring day Rue had been up in Chrissie's room while she was away at school, and found an old shoebox. The shoebox had holes punched in the top. Curious, she was tempted to open it but decided to wait. "I hope she doesn't have a spider in there," thought Rue.

"What do you have in that shoebox in your room?" she asked Chrissie when her daughter got home from school. She knew Chrissie didn't like Rue in her bedroom. "Chrissie, if there's something alive in there, you must let it go immediately." said Rue.

"I'll show you tomorrow," said Chrissie.

The next day they went to her room. But when the box was opened, they both had a surprise. Out came a butterfly! It flew in rapid circles near the ceiling.

Chrissie squealed in surprise, then delight. "It's from the chrysalis I found last fall! When I asked Miss Evans about it a week ago, she said a butterfly might come out anytime!"

"Your teacher was right. We've got to let it go," said Rue.

They opened windows in the bedroom, and waited. After a few minutes, the butterfly found a window and disappeared outside.

One evening, Charles noticed a beautiful sunset. Red, orange, and gold streaked the twilight sky. He called Rue and Chrissie to follow him up to the lighthouse and watch it.

17.

"Isn't that the most beautiful sunset you've ever seen?" he said. Far out on the ocean twinkled the lights of a passing ship. They gazed at the fading dusk until it was gone, and walked quietly back to the house. Vaguely, they knew the fall was coming in. Soon there would be leaves on the ground. Rue stared at the ground and sighed. "It will be getting cold here soon, dear."

Charles looked at his wife and smiled. "Yes, but look at how beautiful the forest will look with all those colors. There will be leaves all over, leaves coming down, falling all around your head. Look up at the sky and see a leaf way up there. Try to catch it. As it comes down."

Rue smiled. She had done exactly that in her childhood. She looked at Chrissie. "Chrissie does that all the time." Rue, Charles, and Chrissie looked at the forest, trying to imagine it bathed in the glowing red, oranges, browns, and reds of the fall colors.

18.

I was dancing when he saw me. I ran and hid....

Chrissie had been dancing with Rags when Raymond spied her. He began to chase her, but she was nimble and ran for a clump of trees. She hid behind a fir with thick branches, but Raymond spotted her.

"Hey, Chrissie! Come out of there, I wanna talk to you," said Raymond.

Chrissie peeked from behind the tree. Before Raymond could walk over, she had climbed up into the lower branches.

"Hey, come down here! I just wanna talk to you," he said.

"I don't trust you, Raymond Black! You just want to pull my hair," said Chrissie.

"Some of the kids say you're weird," said Raymond. "Is it true you talk to a doll?"

"I'm not going to answer that. And if you stay here I'll scream."

"I swear I won't hurt ya."

Suddenly Scott came up behind Raymond. "Hey, Raymond, let's go play marbles," he suggested.

"Guess who I got up a tree. It's Chrissie."

"That kid from the lighthouse? She runs after bugs. She's crazy."

"Hey, ugly, how are you?" taunted both boys.

Chrissie was scared, but knew she musn't show fear; that's what these boys wanted.

"Go away and leave me alone," she said.

"Go 'way? Wouldn't think of it," said Raymond.

"Maybe we should throw rocks at her. That'd get her down quick," said Scott.

Raymond considered this. "Naw, she'd tell her parents. Then we'd be in trouble," said Raymond. "Her papa is the lighthouse keeper."

"Hey, ugly! We'll be back," said Scott. "C'mon, let's go."

Chrissie watched them go, then climbed down from the tree. "Those boys are rotten," she muttered. "Why do they want to hurt me? I've never done anything to them." She looked around. "I'm in the north woods. How did I get here so fast?" At first she felt afraid, but then looked around, shrugged her shoulders and began to walk deeper into the forest. She was curious to see what lay there. Dappled rays of light filtered through the leaves onto the thick bed of pine needles under her feet; the ground felt soft and spongy. She could see toadstools growing near some of the trunks.

"They're fairy chairs," her schoolchum Becky had said. "You know. That's where they sit and have their meetings and stuff." Becky was always talking about fairies flying around, little pixies with wings that glistened like a dragonfly.

Chrissie stared hard at the toadstools, but couldn't see anything resembling fairies.

"Phooey! That Becky is all wet! There's no fairies here." Chrissie looked around. The rays of sunlight were fewer here. Vines and shrubs grew close together; they formed thick masses of foliage that looked dark and strange to her. She thought of the ghost stories the classmate had told her about this place, and decided to go back the way she'd come. She'd explore it another time.

"How did your day go, honey?" asked Rue after Chrissie returned to the lightkeepers house.

"Oh, alright, I guess," said Chrissie.

Rue stared at the diary, crying. "I know you couldn't tell us you'd gone into the north woods, but why didn't you tell me those boys were so mean to you? Why didn't you say something?" she said quietly. The pages of the diary felt damp in her hand; she clutched it tightly and held it close to her bosom.

June 15   Becky taught me how to play marbles today.

Becky had collections of things in her bedroom. She especially liked to collect leaves; her bedroom was full of little boxes where she kept them. She also played marbles. Once in a while, just for fun, she'd challenge the boys to a game.

"C'mon, Chrissie, I'll teach you how to play," Becky had said. So Chrissie sat down with her and learned how to knock an opponent's best marbles out of a circle. One day, during recess, Chrissie had spied Raymond and some other boys playing marbles and decided to join them.

"Go 'way, you're a girl," snarled one boy, whose name was John.

"Yeah, you don't know nuthin' 'bout marbles. What makes you think you can play?" said Raymond.

"Just give me a chance," said Chrissie.

"No! We gave that girl, what's her name, Becky, a chance last week, and she lost! She couldn't shoot worth a darn," said another boy named Matt.

"C'mon, fellas, just one chance, just one quick game," said Chrissie. The boys looked at each other.

"You're pretty pushy," said John. "Alright. One chance, then you're gone, got that?"

"Yes, of course," said Chrissie. She knelt in the dust with the boys.

"Here. And just to show you how nice I am, you get first shot, ugly," said Raymond.

Chrissie felt a surge of anger and looked him square in the eye. "Thanks. But you've got to let me have one deal. If I win, I keep all the marbles."

Raymond laughed. "Yeah, sure. But you ain't gonna win any marbles, so yeah, it's a deal."

Chrissie lined up a marble, and aimed it at the jet-black prize marble she knew belonged to John. Her thumb cocked back and hit the marble dead on. It shot out of her folded fist and square into the black marble, knocking it clean out of the circle.

"Hey! No fair! You had a clear shot!" shouted John. The other boys stared at each other, then at Chrissie.

"Dang, girl! Where'd you learn to shoot like that?" asked Matt.

Chrissie just lined up another marble, took aim, and cleanly shot it out of the circle.

This time Matt and John whistled at her dexterity.

"Good shootin'," said Matt slowly.

A few minutes later, the game was over. Chrissie smiled, and looked at her stash of fifteen marbles. She got up amid the shocked boys and carefully counted all the marbles, made sure to wave the boys' prize marbles in front of the them, and one by one put them into her pocket.

"See ya," she said. When she was out of earshot, she carefully circled back to a spot near the boys, hidden by trees. She wanted to hear what they said.

"Geez," said John. "She's as good as Becky."

Rue stared at the next entry.

I heard Raymond and the others talking about Becky and me. I showed them!

There were a few blank pages. Rue read on, with dread in her heart.

I can't wait to tell Becky, Mama, and Papa!

"Aw, shutup," Raymond had said. "It wouldn't be good if it gets around we got beaten by two girls. Besides, I'm gonna get my marbles back from her. Just you wait. You in with me?"

I'm scared. Raymond said he'd get me for this.

"How you gonna do that?" asked Matt. "What if she beats us again? Then you might lose your silver marble."

Raymond leaned in close to Matt. "'Cause I don't intend to play her. We'll get 'em back another way." The other boys nodded, slowly.

I'll return their marbles. Then I know I'll be okay.

That night, Chrissie had taken the marbles out of her dress pocket. She smiled as she examined each one, especially the two prize marbles belonging to Raymond. Now that she'd taught them a lesson, she'd return all their marbles tomorrow. Chrissie set the marbles down and walked up to her collection of natural objects. She opened one box and took out several bird feathers. She looked at each one, and put them carefully back into the box. Then she reached into a drawer and drew out her prize feather. It was a peacock feather, given to her by Uncle Sidney who'd gotten it somewhere down south, in a place she'd never heard of called San Francisco. He said there was a zoo there filled with strange birds with all kinds of bright feathers. She sighed and put the feather back in the drawer.

Someday I'll show Mama and Papa my whole collection.

The diary entries ended here. Rue slowly turned the remaining moldy, blank pages. Rue clenched her eyes shut, holding onto Chrissie's diary and Raggedy Anne doll.

"I know what happened. I failed you. I let them hurt you."

One warm afternoon, Chrissie had been chasing butterflies. The day was bright and sunny. She sat down on a log to rest. Beside her was a little box full of "objects of curiousity" she'd found that morning. Chrissie opened the box and set the contents down in a small row, examining each thing: a small paper wasp's nest, some seeds, flower petals. She put everything

23.

back into the box. Suddenly she saw a bright yellow butterfly, and ran to chase it. The butterfly was fast and nimble, and Chrissie had trouble keeping up with it. Tired and out of breath, she sat down to rest.

Rue felt fresh tears spilling down her cheeks. "What did they do to you? Tell me what they did to you."

"Well, looky there. If it ain't lil' ol' ugly. Where's my marbles, runt?"

The voice cut through Chrissie. She looked up to see Raymond, John, and Matt walking toward her.

Chrissie got up, spilling the contents of the box on the ground. She started backing up slowly. "I-I don't have them. They're- they're up in my room."

"Well, ugly, hadn't you better go get them?" said Matt.

"I'll bet you've got 'em in your pocket. You just don't want to give 'em back," said Raymond.

Chrissie studied their faces. Matt and John wore frowns, but Raymond looked mean and pitiless. Chrissie had heard of Raymond's reputation at school. He beat up anyone, boy or girl, who crossed him. She should have known better than let him catch her out here.

"I was going to give them back. I'll have to go to the house and get them."

Once again Raymond laughed. "No you ain't. 'Cause if you do, you'll tell your papa, and me and my friends will be in trouble." Raymond glanced sideways at John and Matt. "And we can't let that happen, eh, fellows?"

Matt laughed uncertainly. "Yeah. I'll-I'll bet you've got them marbles in your pocket. If you do, maybe we'll only hit you once."

Raymond laughed again. "Naw. This uppity runt needs at least a couple of slaps. And after that, unless she wants more, she'd better shut up about it."

Suddenly there was a swoosh, and a flock of birds flew up from the trees.

Chrissie took this moment to start running as fast as she could. Before the surprised boys could recover, she'd sprinted fifty feet ahead, towards a clump of trees.

"Get her," yelled Raymond, "she's headed towards the north woods, and we might lose her."

"Give it up, ugly," shouted Matt. "You can't get away from us."

Chrissie ran as fast as she could go. She didn't think about the trees getting closer and the light darker; she was panting, running her hardest, her dress and apron flying up around her. She didn't see the cistern until she was on its edge, and then it was too late. Her parents, sitting in the house, didn't hear her agonized shriek as she fell in.

"Did you hear that?" said John.

"Nope. Why? What'd it sound like?" asked Raymond.

"It sounded like a scream or something."

"Didn't hear nothing." said Raymond. "You hear anything?" he asked Matt.

"Yeah, I..I think it sounded like somebody yelling, but I'm not sure."

The boys searched for a few minutes.

"It's too dark in here. Let's go," said Matt.

"So where's the runt?" asked John.

"Who knows? Who cares," said Raymond. "If she fell and got hurt it'd serve her right. It's too damn dark to search for her anyway. I'm goin'."

The boys left.

In two hours, when Chrissie failed to come home, people from both lightkeeper houses started searching for her. They spread out in groups of twos to look. It was one boy from the assistant keeper's house who glanced down the cistern and saw Chrissie's white dress. He yelled and ran for help. Closeby, they found the spilled objects Chrissie had collected.

Rue fainted and had to be calmed with laudenum. All the next day she sat in shock, unable to move. After a short funeral service, Chrissie's body was carried to the deep woods between the lighthouse and the keeper's houses and buried.

The families gathered in silence. Rue was distraught.

"You didn't fix that cistern in time," she cried. "Why? Why?"

Charles couldn't answer her. Rue would not be comforted. That night, she couldn't sleep, and the next morning had developed a fever. The fever grew worse, and Rue became very sick. A doctor was summoned, but it would take him several hours to get there because of the distance and muddy roads.

"My darling, my darling, what have they done to you?" murmured Rue feverishly, tossing and turning under the blankets. "I want to see her again, now," she said to Charles.

"I will take you to her," he said. They walked in silence up the hill and stood over the grave. There were vases filled with flowers all around the little temporary marker.

"It's beautiful here. Chrissie would love this place." said Rue quietly.

That evening Rue was looking through Chrissie's room, and found her small diary. It was in a drawer, tucked behind Rag's pinafore. She picked them up, put them in a drawer downstairs, and locked it.

The boys had confessed to chasing Chrissie. Raymond said he'd had nothing to do with Chrissie falling into the cistern, and was finally let go.

In a week a stone arrived from Florence with Chrissie's name on it that was placed flat faceup over the grave.

Years went by. Lighthouse families came and went. The lighthouse remained, lighting the way for lost mariners. In 1930, electricity came to Heceta Head, and there was no more need for three lightkeepers. In 1940, the headkeepers house was torn down. Now only the assistant lightkeeper's house still stood. In the 1940's a new highway, 101, was built, allowing easy access to Heceta Head. The cows and chickens were sold off because new food markets were being built, and there was no need to raise or keep farm animals. The lighthouse families were fewer now, and in 1963 the lighthouse was fully automated with electricity, eliminating light-keepers completely.

Rue started out of her reverie, staring around her. The shadows on the wall had deepened, which could mean but one thing; it was late in the day. She glanced out the attic window; the sun was settling over the ocean. She looked down. The doll was still clenched in one hand, the diary in the other. Placing both diary and doll into the drawer, she carefully closed it.

One day a contractor came up into the attic to replace a broken window. He carried a big sack full of tools, and grabbing a hammer, proceeded to pound noisily.

"He's probably up to no good," thought Rue, eyeing him suspiciously. She came over to have a closer look, but when the workman saw her, he yelled in terror and fled.

Rue was sad about this, and sent him dreams for the next several nights in which she implored him to come back.

"Please come back and finish your job," she begged. "I'm sorry I frightened you. Please come back." He eventually did...but not to the attic. He came back to put the window in from the outside...and promptly broke one of the panes. Shards of glass fell onto the attic floor.

"I made a mistake," Rue thought, surveying the broken glass. "He was a skilled carpenter. Now what shall I do?" Sighing, she reached over into the corner, picked up a broom, and carefully swept the pieces of glass into a neat pile. On the floor below, people heard the sound of sweeping, and looked with fear at the ceiling. But Rue was just being neat and tidy; she didn't like to leave messes in her house.

She went down to the beach one day and saw a group of children playing in the distance. Rue made herself invisible and drew nearer to them. She looked the children over carefully, and realized they were unfamiliar to her. They were also wearing strange clothing. When she went up to the lighthouse there were more families, but they were all strangers. She looked out over the railing to the sea and a picture flashed into her mind of a sunset that she had seen long ago, of a sky with bright yellow-orange light fading to a deep red and purple. "Where are the children I knew? It seems they lived in another life." She went outside and sat down to think.

One day a woman wearing a strange dress arrived at the house. It looked like something out of the past, but was nothing Rue recognized. She looked out the window at the falling leaves and wondered if there was some important celebration going on. It had been a warm, sunny fall day, one that filled her with longing and sadness. More people arrived dressed in outlandish clothes; there was a ballerina, a pirate, and a cowboy. Rue looked behind her and gasped. There was another woman dressed exactly like her! She wore an identical white blouse with a pendant and a long black skirt.

"I'll ask her," thought Rue. "Maybe she knows what's going on here." She was about to walk forward when a man came up behind the woman and kissed her. Rue stopped and stared at him. He looked like a Roman Centurion. She wondered what on earth could be happening.

29.
Glancing at a calendar she saw the date was October 31. Dimly she was aware that something important was supposed to happen on that day, but she couldn't remember what it was. Then

she heard someone say, 'Halloween.' "Halloween! Oh my goodness! Oh, yes!" Rue cried aloud.

"It's Halloween!" There was the sound of laughter. Rue glanced at more people arriving.

"We're going to have a seance tonight," said the pirate, whose name was Tom.

"What for?" asked Belinda, the ballerina.

"To contact the spirit that lives here," said Tom.

The cowboy, whose name was James, came over. "Great! There's a spook here?"

"Supposedly," said Tom. "I don't believe in ghosts, but we'll try."

Rue wondered who on earth the spirit was. She had dim memories of Halloween family parties long ago with bobbing for apples and dressing up the children as ghosts.

A real ghost?" she thought. "Who is it? I wonder what it looks like?" She decided to

join in the fun. The seance got underway in a few minutes, with Tom, Belinda, James, a witch named Sylvia, and an older woman named Mary dressed as a clown.

Sylvia brought out an Ouija board. "Let's see if the spirit says anything." she said. She set the board flat on a coffee table and backed away from it.

"Who are you?" she asked. Rue smiled and walked over to the woman. She remembered stories of Ouija boards, how they were often used by charlatans to hoodwink people. Playfully, she spelled out the letters R-U-E.

"Oh my goodness, it's really working, look! It's spelled someone's name!" cried Belinda.

The others crowded around. "Let's join hands."

"Oh, spirit Rue," said Sylvia, "if you can hear us, rap three times under the table."

"They'd only know it was a joke," thought Rue, reaching her hand under the table. Playfully, she rapped three times. Everyone gasped.

"Oh, spirit Rue, if that really is you, rap just once under the table," said Sylvia.

This time Rue decided to rap fifteen times.

"I think the spirit is confused," said Belinda.

"Rue, what do you want? Where are your husband and children?" asked a bold Mary.

At this mention of Charles and Chrissie tears flowed down Rue's cheeks.

"I hear someone crying!" exclaimed Belinda.

They all looked at each other and shook their heads.

Rue saw a piece of paper and pencil. She snatched them up and began writing furiously.

"Rue, is that really you?" began Sylvia again. "Do you have something to say?"

Rue leaned over the group of people, and dropped the piece of paper. It floated down like a white dove, landing squarely in the middle of them. Sylvia opened the piece of paper. Inside were scrawled the words, MY DAUGHTER. HELP ME FIND HER.

"What's that on the paper?" asked Mary, pointing to some stains.

Sylvia studied the stains closely. "I don't know, but I could swear they're tears," she said.

She suddenly jerked her head up. Something wet had hit her on the shoulder.

She reached out and touched the tip of one stain with her fingertip. "I think it's a tear. Can a ghost cry?"

James had a sudden inspiration. "Rue, your daughter is out there. She's out there right now, waiting for you."

Rue shook her head. "My daughter is dead. I don't even know where she's buried now."

James spoke again. "She's out there, alive, I know it."

Rue felt a sudden anger. "I tell you, she's dead...!" she started to shout.

Suddenly there was a squeal of childish laughter, and a flash of white raced past the window! Rue stared open-mouthed for a second, then jumped up and glided through the wall. Outside she looked around wildly. The little girl came into view. She was giggling, wearing a white bonnet and matching dress. A butterfly fluttered just in front of her, and the child strove to keep up with it. Her figure shone for an instant in front of a line of dark trees, then was swallowed up in the forest.

Rue's struggled to say something, but no words would come out. The child was running into the north woods! A whimper from Rue finally forced itself out in a scream.

"The cistern. Dear God, STOP, STOP!" Rue ran into the woods. She looked frantically ahead, but couldn't see anything. The child giggled in the gloom, but Rue couldn't tell which direction. It was very dark under the trees, and she strained to see around her. "Where are you? Please, dear God, tell me where you are." The laughter came again from her left and there was the little girl! She was running way ahead of Rue, off to the side. She stopped for a second and looked back at Rue smiling, turned and continued to run farther into the woods!

"Look out," screamed Rue. "The Cistern! No, No!"

Suddenly the little girl stopped. She turned around, and began walking back towards Rue.

33.

"Mama?" she said. "I'm alright. There's no cistern here anymore."

Rue ran up to the little girl.

I'm alright," the child said, looking up at her. It was Chrissie!

Rue fell on her knees, and clasped her arms tightly around her daughter. "Chrissie. You've come back to me."

"I've never been gone. If you keep me in your heart, I'll always be there, Mama," Chrissie said.

"But is it really you? You're not a dream?" sobbed Rue.

"No Mama, it's me. And we're never going to be apart again. Papa's here too."

"Ruth."

Rue turned around, and there stood Charles! He looked young and handsome, not the old man she had last known him as.

Charles smiled, and held out his arms. "Chrissie and I have come to take you home." Charles turned and pointed at something towards the lighthouse. He began walking up the hill, Rue and Chrissie following on either side. Charles led them to the western guardrail, and looked out over the edge.

"Isn't that the most beautiful sunset you've ever seen?"

"Oh, yes, Papa, it is beautiful," declared Chrissie.

"Charles, it is beautiful," whispered Rue quietly. "And the sea looks so still."

"Ruth, take my hand. Are you ready?"

"Yes, dear, I'm ready," said Rue, her face shining with joy.

"I'm ready, Papa," cried Chrissie, taking her father's other hand.

"Now we must walk forward," said Charles.

Slowly, as they walked forward, their shapes dissolved into the oranges and reds of the twilight sky and melted into the dark brown of the earth below.

The next morning dawned quietly. The sun rose slowly into a deep blue sky that foretold a day of tranquility and calm. Children played on the grass, chasing each other in the warm autumn sunshine.

A butterfly suddenly flew across the childrens' path, and one little girl went to chase it. The butterfly flew higher, and the little girl watched it become smaller until it disappeared into the turquoise sky.

EPILOGUE

Thirteen miles to the north of Florence, Oregon, sits Heceta Head Lighthouse. There are some who say a ghost of unknown origin named "Rue" still haunts the lightkeepers house. Others who know better say they no longer feel her presence. There are some who say there is the long-forgotten grave of a little girl somewhere between the lightkeeper's house and lighthouse, location unknown, and probably covered with grass and bushes. But whether Rue is there or not, those who understand say on a day in autumn her heart found peace.

The End

Author Tom Romano is the author of three other books, *Birds of Prey and Other Endangered Species*, *Jeweled Travelers of the Skies,* and *Creatures of the World.* These first three are self-written nature books for children. *The Watcher in the Lighthouse* is his fourth book. In addition, Mr. Romano has collaborated with other authors in illustrating their bookcovers. He illustrated the *Pamela 13* series for author Patricia Lee Strunk, *Demon Ridge* by C.I. Kemp, and *El Sentir de una Mujer Cubana* by Cuban American author Eloina Marquez. Mr. Romano does all of his own illustrations for his children's books. He currently lives in Eugene, Oregon with a cat.